Renate Weldi
Lived Moments
Poems
Volume 1

Renate Weldi

Lived Moments

Poetry of everyday life

Imprint

Bibliographic Information of the German National Library: The German National Library lists this publication in the German National Bibliography; detailed bibliographic data can be accessed online at http://dnb.dnb.de.

Publisher: BoD · Books on Demand GmbH, Überseering 33, 22297 Hamburg, bod@bod.de

Printing: Libri Plureos GmbH, Friedensallee 273, 22763 Hamburg

ISBN: 978-3-8192-7629-3

Thanks to:

My mother Magdalena Weldi
My friend Ricky Chan
My friend Marie
My friend Renate Martsch
And all crowfounding participants who made this project possible.

Foreword

Poems emerged in the moment of authentic experience. Today, they would probably be called poems of mindfulness. They reflect that life is full of unique, precious moments - but challenges are also part of it. It is precisely these challenges that open up new perspectives for us and foster our inner growth. In the end, it is these experiences that shape us and make us into the person we have become.

Show me life and humanity in all their colors.

Everything that exists has a deeply rooted justification for being. Nothing happens without reason; nothing is arbitrary. Every living being, every human, even the smallest detail of life is an expression of a higher order and therefore deserves our unconditional respect and deepest reverence.

That is why we should approach everything around us - whether visible or hidden, familiar or foreign - with humility, appreciation, and devotion. Everything contributes to the unfolding of our consciousness; everything is part of a greater whole. Only when we learn to see with open eyes, an open mind, and an open heart can we recognize the true nature of life.

The Flight

How paradoxical it seems
That madness and knowledge unite in our dreams.
The madness of sitting in tons of heavy steel,
Yet the knowledge that here I can sit and feel at peace.
To rise into the open sky,
And take in the view from a bird's eye.
I fly and marvel at myself,
For knowledge and trust are a steadfast shelf.
Above me, the sky - blue and clear,
Below me, the clouds, so close and near.
What a wonder - this heavy, steel-bound machine,
In which we place trust where elsewhere it would seem obscene.
Within me rises the truth - we want to trust
What serves us well and expands our view - we must.
Trust strengthens the wavering heart,
Through new perspectives, we gather knowledge - a fiery start.

My own photography

The Atom

Atom so small
And yet the building block of all.
You are built like a solar array,
Electrons and protons the planets, the nucleon the sun in play.
Billions of atoms - that's you and me.
So much movement inside, never still or free.
Electrons rushing eagerly around,
To grasp that truth is truly sound.
We are not fixed, not rigidly made,
If you take a closer gaze.
Solid matter is an illusion, you see -
That's what the old physicists would agree.
(At least what we call "solid" in our mind
Has no real part in humankind.)
Energy is all, and movement inside,
That's what gives change and life their guide.
So use the energy that you possess!
Don't let lethargy make it less.

Image created by A.I.

The Bird

I sit, thinking of nothing, on the balcony,
When, like a flash, a joyful tone strikes me.
In the hedge before me hops a tiny sprite,
Unassuming, with a face so sweet and light.
I don't know you.
You haven't introduced yourself, little bird, it's true.
Yet you hop joyfully from branch to branch,
And sing a song - I am your guest by chance.
The song fills my chest with bliss,
I'd love to join in, singing with eagerness.
But I fear to rise or make a sound,
It might quickly bring your song to ground.
So I sit still, completely fulfilled,
Listening to the song that touches my spirit and will.
Who sent you here? Did you somehow know
That I arrived here weary and low?
You won't allow it - you sing and sing,
And slowly, deep joy to my heart you bring.
Thank you, dear little bird, so small and bright,
For helping me recover with your song's pure light.

Imagine created by A.I.

The Spider

In a corner, dust motes dance in the light.
A spider sits within, weaving a web like a poem's flight.
Threads of silk, delicate and fine, flow from her slender frame,
Forming a wheel of spokes, she climbs the rungs without shame.
An inner plan, who would have thought,
Guides her - each knot carefully wrought.
Diligently, the spider moves,
And yet how fleeting is the work she proves.
With devotion and courage, she dances this thread,
While the light reflects the beauty of silk that's spread.
As she weaves, I think of the threads of my dreams,
The paths they create, the edges they seem.
The spider spins on - this is her world,
And I marvel at the simplicity that keeps it unfurled.
So, too, the threads and knots of my dreams,
Creating new spaces where reality gleams.

My own photography

Asparagus

Spring awakens with mighty power,
On the fields, asparagus sprouts soft as a flower.
But without bitterness, I cannot delight,
For without that edge, no dish feels quite right.
The vegetable stands proud and fine,
Yet without bitterness, it's not truly mine.
It tastes bland, lacking edge and flair,
A truth I once was unaware.
For in bitterness sometimes lies the spice,
Just like in life - to put it precise.

Imagine created by A.I.

The Kaleidoscope

A kaleidoscope of vibrant hue,
Is humankind, so full of life and true.
Respect and care are what we owe,
Accepting each being, letting them grow.
The uniqueness of every single soul
Is like a special shade that makes them whole.
The tears and laughter along their way
Shape a work of art in their own display.
Thus, the kaleidoscope of humankind spins around,
Quietly painting colors that truly astound.
Let us admire and understand each face,
And see the beauty in their unique space.
From countless fragments, shades, and light,
The kaleidoscope of humankind takes flight.
What richness! What strength! A sight so vast,
A masterpiece of colors meant to last.

Imagine created by A.I.

My Garden

I dig my hands into you deep,
And in that moment, my whole self I keep.
Your scent that brushes against my nose
Carries me back to childhood's repose.
Suddenly, like the earthworm, quick to hide,
While I harvest a radish with quiet pride.
You fragrant soil, to us you are given
To nourish and bless us - a gift from heaven.
The fresh green lettuce sparks an idea anew
Of what will later lie in view.
The beetroot grows stronger day by day;
Watching it brings peace and takes stress away.
The humming of bees surrounds me still
As I work the earth with love and will.
You, Earth, were given for our care,
A foundation for plants, animals, humans - life everywhere.

My own photography

The Half-Timbered House
In Linkenheim-Hochstetten (Germany)

I'm sitting here, doing nothing,
So I'm just writing this poem for something.
I'm on a break with nothing to say,
And nothing to complain about today.
In front of me stands a cup of good coffee,
Not far from here lies also a lake.
But going there wouldn't be worth the ride
The atmosphere here is a poem inside.
The little café is dreamy and bright;
I haven't seen such coziness in quite some nights.
Thirty more minutes, then the break is through -
Spending it here wasn't a foolish thing to do.

Now it's quiet, restful, and fine,
In thirty minutes, I'll dive back into the grind.
But this pause here gives me strength anew.

Imagine provided by the „Fachwerkhaus" in Linkenheim-Hochstetten (Germany)

Free - Time

The silence around me is calm and free.
Peace surrounds me; I feel carefree.
In the background, appointments and challenges await.
I've heard their call, I know their weight.
But I let them wait with patient grace,
As I now work calmly in this place.
I leave the pressure where it stands,
It cannot seize me with its hands.
I enjoy the life that surrounds me now,
And that brings a smile to my brow.
I let my worries drift away,
And use my time in a mindful way.
This moment brings me peace at last,
Letting go of everything that's passed.
Now I let the moment carry me,
May this calmness always be.
The answers will wait till I am ready-
That's the purpose of a pause that's steady.
In this state of rest and ease,
I feel the freedom on this breeze.
I live the here and now with care,
Drawing calmness from the air.
Amidst the chaos, now I'm free,
Enjoying life without misery.
What a gift that I've been given,
To feel these moments, deeply driven.

My own photography

Sleep

Fatigue grips my limbs,
My heavy eyelids long to sink.
The stars in the sky, they shine so bright,
Like scattered pearls, a wondrous sight.
Dreams begin to softly knock,
Wishing to lure me to another world.
The ocean of calm now spreads wide,
I sink into it, take it in stride.
The peace that's here now, the peace of the night,
Accompanies me until morning light.
I rest and let the night guide me,
Leading me toward new times to see.
The day is done, now past and gone,
What happened today can't be undone.
After this night, so calm and deep,
Tomorrow I'll wake from peaceful sleep.
I'll greet the new day and start anew,
Without dwelling on what I once knew.
Now you too sleep,
In peaceful, quiet, slumber deep.

Imagine created by A.I.

The Victory

On the way forward, you are not fast enough for the others.
Not clever enough.
They scream, they push, they shove and they curse.
You can't climb the mountain fast enough.
You must learn to block it out,
Make your steps steady, turn toward your goal with calm.
When the path becomes steep and sharply ascends,
No one is there to cheer you on.
Instead, they sit comfortably in their chairs,
Reflecting on your path and passing judgment.
You haven't made it yet, you haven't conquered the mountain.
Surely, they think, you've run away and fled.
You take the last hurdle, the victory is near -
Now suddenly they all join in and shout: Hurrah!
After all, they had bet on the right horse.
The victory belongs to them - you are worth nothing anymore.
You stand alone now at the summit's cross,
Empty, disappointed, tired - just wanting to rest.
They honor you now,
But it means nothing anymore.
Where you once faced misery alone,
Where you hesitated, unsure which path to take,
Where your strength threatened to give out,
Where you were in bitter distress,
There you stood alone; no one cared.
They turned away, left you behind.
But now you are here,
Alone and so close
To the truth of all victors,
The realization of all high-flyers:
Victory makes you lonely
Because the path is rarely walked together.
Only discipline and a clear conscience
Help in the end to raise the banner of victory.
So remember this above all:
Only clear decisions and the courage to face solitude bring true victory.

Imagine created by A.I.

The Vacation Is Over

Tired, still a few hours to wait
Before I can finally start heading home.
Like a cloud hovering over me,
My thoughts now swirl around me.
I'm already thinking about everything, though I'm not there yet,
And I'm already caught up in the plan.
Work, training, finances, and you —
It's all weaving my head shut now.
I push the confusion away from me,
Take one thing at a time and think it through.
Then I set my priorities —
That's essential, it's the only way it works.
Isn't it tough and frustrating
That I'm sacrificing the last day like this?
But I want to arrive prepared
And that remains unquestioned.
I know that when I land and get home,
Work will be waiting and hasn't gone anywhere.
I'm known for my reliability,
So I waste no time.
The last day is loathsome to me,
It prepares me anew for my burden.

My own photography

Restful Day in High Summer

Just yesterday, it was unbearably hard.
Not a single leaf stirred on the trees.
The humid heat hung over us,
How we longed for a breath of wind.
Every person, every creature groaned,
Yearning for refreshment and restful pleasure.
Then the storm came late in the evening,
It was invigorating and uplifting.
Slowly, the lukewarm breeze
Turned cooler, refreshing, pleasant.
In the morning, I woke up early,
After a truly revitalizing night.
The sun shines, the air is cool.
What a glorious, pleasant feeling!
The birds are chirping, newly revived,
At the horizon, a tower of clouds rises.
Then it begins - thunder and lightning,
Raindrops falling, nature delighting.
How everything had longed to experience it.
That restful, so missed rain.
Now the fresh air surrounds us,
Giving restful breath and new strength.
A magic, a wonder is this air,
Infused with the scent of cool rain.

My own photography

Refreshing Change of Weather

The sun burns hot, the air feels heavy,
No hope for relief around me, not any.
The sky before me still shines bright and blue,
When, surprised, I spot the first drop breaking through.
The joy that slowly fills human hearts,
As raindrops begin their dancing arts.
The air is pierced by a newfound breeze,
While I sit here, feeling at ease.
On the terrace beside my home,
I sip my coffee, content and alone.
Now I sit here, breathing deep,
The fresh, cool air that starts to creep.
An early morning, the rain brings relief and bliss,
As I savor my breakfast in peacefulness.
The air was so heavy, so thick before,
Now it feels light, a gift I adore.
The drought retreats, the land renews,
A touch of magic in calming hues.
Gratefully smiling, I watch the rain flow,
Enjoying my coffee. Both a perfect glow.

My own photography

Aging

The moment when you realize how old you really are -
it doesn't disturb you.
It sets you free
From all worries, from all time.
I know, this is me, today and here.
That gives light, I like it.
What lies behind, I have overcome.
I truly don't need to regret it.
Life has taught me a lot.
And that alone is the goal.
That I have achieved this now shows itself
In a liberated laugh, an inner celebration.

Artwork painted by my friend Renate Martsch

Breaking Down the Walls Within

My gaze drifts freely, forward and back.
My heart suddenly wide and full of luck.
For now, right here, I've taken the time
And found my way back to myself, aligned.
My gaze glides far over the sea,
No more boundaries holding me.
Sky and ocean tightly embraced,
As seagulls sing their song with grace.
The weather remains the same.
This freedom endlessly rich to claim.
Shamelessly blue on glorious days,
Dark gray when winds sweep it away.
Now the air is soaked and dense
With the seaweed's salty scent.
What strength! What energy!
So often forgotten by humanity - what irony!
This pleasure is gifted to us for free.
The power of nature, this wild ecstasy.
Yet so often we remain blind to it,
Trapped in our minds, stuck in the pit.
The walls we build them ourselves.
Life feels hard, or so we tell.
But look around and finally see:
What truly matters is infinity.
Open your eyes, your mind, step off the worn track!
Refuel for free the wisdom, the joy, the strength of nature's knack.

Imagine created by A.I.

Carefree

Amidst the silence, relaxed and free,
Surrounded by calm - I feel carefree.
Although problems linger in the background,
I can let them go, just move on unbound.
The appointments wait patiently behind,
But now I'm free, refusing to be confined.
Calmly, I smile at this peaceful state,
In this moment, life feels truly great.
I let the worries drift away, breathe in deep.
This moment could not be more complete.
Time belongs to me; I use it with care,
Refueling my strength in the present air.
My thoughts flow gently, like a stream,
Carrying me onward, light as a dream.
Peace surrounds this quiet space,
As the world around me fades without a trace.
So I let myself be carried by ease,
With no reason to fear or appease.
If problems won't wait or time's hard to find,
Let them simply vanish from my mind.
Problems will come, but they also will go.
I've seen this pattern enough to know.
Today, I have no time for despair.
Today belongs to pause and self-care.
If tomorrow the problems remain in sight,
I'll face them calmly in tomorrow's light.
But right now, in this calm and restful view,
I feel inner freedom breaking through.
Amidst the chaos, I'm relaxed and free.
Whatever tomorrow brings means nothing to me.

Loneliness or Being Alone

Being alone is silence, peace, and growth,
Giving the soul space and strengthening inner poise.
Loneliness, on the other hand, is heavy,
There is a pain that gnaws at the heart, a deep ache.
Being alone is a choice, a quiet space,
A place to live out your own dream.
Thoughts that flow like a gentle stream,
Here you are free from every frustration.
Loneliness is a heavy garment,
Worn with tears and deep sorrow.
The soul seeks warmth but finds none,
Tears burn as they moisten a sad face.
The silence of being alone brings freedom you attain.
Loneliness cries out for company, filled with painful fear.
Being alone is rich, restorative, and always strengthens you.
Loneliness robs you of the right path.

(Also published in the Frankfurt Library 2025 Edition, page 362)

You Four, You

You and you and you and you,
And all I want is peace, it's true.
Because what I need, you cannot give,
Nor do you look honestly at how I live.
You only want to steal my energy,
To force me down onto my knees.
So I tell you, and you, and you, and you:
Keep going your way - but I'm through.
I know what I need, and that's enough,
I'm grown now, wise and tough.
To be happy, I don't need you near.
I am enough for myself, that's clear.
I love nature, I love to roam,
It lets me walk alone - that's home.
You want sex when it suits you best,
Believe me, that kind of love I detest.
You want me to handle the housework too,
But that's not why I came to you.
You only ever talk about yourself.
But that alone won't fill my shelf.
What I need now is crystal clear:
No one to lead me to the altar, dear.

To share things, side by side,
To listen, not just let it slide.
To be there sometimes : me for you,
And just as much you for me too.

Imagine created by A.I.

Waiting

Waiting...- is the art of being.
Waiting…- must be done alone, without fleeing.
Waiting…- it's so hard to bear.
Waiting…- I don't want it anymore.
Waiting…- who will teach it to me?
Waiting…- it's a burden for you and me.
Waiting…- I really dislike it, I swear.
Waiting…- the highest art to be aware.
And yet, when I really reflect,
Waiting…- has held meaning since childhood, in retrospect.
Waiting…- filled with so much hope,
Waiting…- where anticipation helps you cope.
Waiting…- a chance to pause and think.
Waiting…- so rich, a gift on the brink.
Waiting…- grants a fresh new view,
On everything we've already been through.
Waiting…- it shapes and changes the way,
Waiting…- learned means I won't walk away.
Waiting…- when I think it through,
Waiting…- is a precious gift too.

Imagine created by A.I.

My Dark Companion

A breath away from me, you walk by my side.
I think how beautiful life would be without you.
I don't look at you, don't acknowledge you.
I turn away and face the light.
But you are there.
You're so close to me.
Watching me, never leaving me.
Not even when I strive toward the light.
A victory achieved, joy is here…
You speak up, you're close to me.
Tears wet my eyes,
And pure terror rises within me.
Just when I least expect it,
You play your ace card.
You don't say a word,
Yet you want to devour me, Depression.
Escaped again.
Crawled out of the hole.
Fighting back doesn't help here,
But facing you consciously does.
Okay, it seems you'll always walk beside me.
But the boss of my life - that's me alone.

Imagine created by A.I.

Blue

Blue in so many shades,
A gentle touch caressing my soul.
The sound of the ocean, the sun on my skin -
How long has my longing been bottled within.
Now I am here.
The Mediterranean lies before me.
The blue, the turquoise, the sun to savor.
Tomorrow, a few drops shall water the earth.
Fully present in the here and now,
Everything else fades away somehow.
The white foam crowns pouring from the blue of the sea
Make me forget the rest of the world entirely.
The warm breeze gently surrounds me,
While the sun burns down from the sky.
The sea is still cool, and the refreshing water revives me.
One more short break, then I'll go to the table to dine.

An original oil painting on canvas (60 x 80 cm) painted by myself – Renate Weldi

Hiking in Mallorca

After a lot of sleep, I've woken at last.
My tiredness finally left me last night, so fast.
Fresh, happy, and free, I sip my coffee,
Now I start my hike about two hours, hopefully.
Everything's empty.
No one yet at the sea.
I hike to south along the coast,
Through sand on the beach - a tiring post.
The air is still fresh, but the sun starts to burn,
While waves thunder, racing toward the shore in return.
I pass from viewpoint to beautiful scene,
The rocks on the shore shape pictures, serene.
The sound of the waves deeply relaxes my mind.
I walk alone, self-reliant, unconfined.
Planning, deciding, changing my route,
Free from concern, no need to take another's view.
When to go, how far, where to steer -
I decide alone; that's why I'm here.
Freeing for mind, soul, and body alike,
Following my own rhythm that's what makes me truly rich.

My own photography

Hike to Son Real (Mallorca)

Awake.
The view from the window awakens desire
for what I have planned for this day.
I will hike along the sea, just the way I like it.
Then off I go!
Off to the path!
I take the route shown by the app,
surprised, because the sand shows no trace of it.
Aha - so this is how it is, the training will be a bit harder.
The grains of sand grip every step a little tighter.
The wind is still cool and caresses my skin,
while the sun shines down on me, marveling at me.
The sea foams loudly as it crashes onto the shore.
In this moment, the land seems empty of people.
High above me, a seagull flies.
Far on the horizon, a ship rests on the sea.
The scent of seaweed penetrates my chest.
Every frustration lies far behind me.
So I walk on at my own pace,
enjoying nature. A refreshing emptiness fills me.
I don't think,
not like I usually do, day after day.
I savor the solitude and the nature.
That is what I need; it is my cure.
Again and again, I quickly snap a photo.
I see great and small wonders they brighten my soul.
Now I've arrived at the necropolis,
admiring the ancient structures.
Who were you?
Why here of all places?
On the edge of the cliffs, directly by the sea,
you said your goodbyes. Now the graves are empty.
How did you live in your century?

My own photography

It was 700 BC, they have found out.
What was nature like in your time?
I didn't read up on it. I wasn't prepared.
Should I question you in the coming days?
Would you be willing to tell me everything about your life?
A shame. Thoughtfully, I turn back
toward the hiking path.
I sit down on a rock
and ask myself: what were your songs like back then?
I apply sunscreen, drink a little,
grateful and happy for the refreshing coolness.
I move on, forward - it was beautiful this time,
at the necropolis of Son Real.
I walk a little further,
enjoying nature, then turn back.
On the way back, I meet now and then
people heading toward Son Real.
I discover astonishing things along the path I had already taken,
and yet I had missed so much.
The dwelling cave - I only notice it now.
I hadn't seen it on the way out.
It's very small.
Was it a shelter, a home?
How wonderful it feels to wander
from one discovery to another.
The colors of the sea, the mountain on the horizon -
they change hourly. That is true art.
The wind caresses my skin.
The sun embraces me, gives me strength.
Why am I always waiting for someone to share this with me?
That is, in truth, just wasted time.
Every attempt I've made to share this
has cost me freedom and led nowhere.
Better to be free and alone
than unfulfilled and bound.

My own photography

A Rock by the Sea

I sit here, doing nothing at all.
A poem forms within my mind's hall.
The rock beneath me gives me stead,
While the waves' roar echoes in my head.
The sea's display of colors - shamelessly bright.
How could I possibly leave such a sight?
The sea has filled me with strength and delight,
So I will leave again, feeling light.
Turquoise expanses framed with blue,
The surface foamed with white in view,
Where the waves break close to the sand.
Enthralled, I watch this natural stand.
I'm still here now,
But in my heart somehow
Grows the longing to always be near,
To you, dear sea, feeling safe and clear.
For the wind and the waves have taken my stress,
And left me whole, not feeling less.
I am not one who lies on the shore.
Nor one who builds on sand anymore.
I am one who seeks to live aware,
Embracing the breaks that life lays bare.
While the waves scatter roses around,
I let sun and wind wrap me, unbound.
Sitting on a rock, surrounded by nature's pure,
I savor this moment - simple, secure.

My own photography

Riddle

It's raining and I have the day off.
What to do? Suddenly, an idea rushes by.
Full of excitement, I hurry to you.
Today, I am food for you.
I arrive in no time,
Full of energy,
I pay at the counter,
So you can nibble on me right away.
Feet washed, one, two, three.
You're already waiting. I dip my feet into the blue water.
The crowd rushes toward my feet,
As if they were starving.
They suck, nibble,
Tickle, hasten.
All I think is:
Once again, a wonder of nature.
For everything we need in life,
Nature has given us a solution.

Now say it quickly, where was I?

At the fish spa, not at the bar.

My own photography

Hiking to Lake Zurich and Back

For so long I've yearned for this,
To walk uphill and down in bliss.
Passion and peace, that's what hiking brings,
From one place to another, my soul takes wings.
To walk alone, to feel nature's touch,
Gives strength, brings calm, it means so much.
The path I've chosen, rugged and steep,
A challenge for sure, but promises deep.
I set off now, free of weight,
No rush, no pressure - a perfect state.
No one waits, and nothing calls.
That's the secret to peaceful walls.
Through Swiss towns, I make my way,
It seems as though all life's away.
But quietly in each garden creeps
An electronic beetle that tirelessly keeps
Mowing the grass without a rest,
Neatly trimming, doing its best.
I pass through village after town,
Until below me I finally look down -
Lake Zurich, still and shy,
Bathed in sunlight, hot and dry.
I walk on until I stand
At the viewpoint, where the lake meets land.
The ducks are splashing in cool delight,
Swans are diving, searching for a bite.
Boats rest lazily by the pier,
Only one ship cuts the water, clear.

My own photography

It's so quiet, nothing meets my ears.
The lapping waves, the buzzing near.
I breathe in deep - here and now,
I've reached my goal, I take a bow.
I turn around, surprised to see
A lizard gazing straight at me.
Eye to eye - what a gift.
A fleeting moment, a gentle shift.
It's easy going down to the lake,
But climbing back up - my legs will ache!
I stop for a rest at a small café,
Eat and refresh before heading away.
Upward again, the sun beats down,
Sweat dripping beneath my crown.
At a forest playground, I surrender,
Lie on a bench, let thoughts grow tender.
How long I rest - I do not care,
Today's a day free from despair.
Grateful thoughts of those I love,
Who give me the freedom I'm dreaming of.
Refreshed, I stand, though my feet protest:
"Please, not more - give us a rest!"
I gently coax them, "Just a bit more,
Soon we'll rest, I'm sure."
Back home at last, my heart feels light,
Content and glowing with pure delight.
A glass of fresh water in my hand -
Today was a gift, simple and grand.

My own photography

Rhine Falls at Schaffhausen

I have often seen the Rhine Falls at Schaffhausen,
Yet in my soul, wishes stir anew.
Today I pass by and have the time
To fulfill them - what a delight!
But in the morning, as I start my day,
The rain seems to wash my plans away.
So I set off, sad and alone,
Once again not stopping at the Rhine.
Suddenly, near the longed-for place,
The clouds are gone, the sun lights my face.
So I take the exit without hesitation
And arrive at the Rhine Falls with elation.
I book the ride to the falls' rocky heart,
And watch the ducks and catfish dart.
Now the boat approaches its goal,
The roaring flood knows no control.
The boat groans, struggling to stay,
So it can let us step off and stray.
The spray refreshes like warm rain,
The force of the torrents surrounds the terrain.
I marvel at this uncanny might,
That the water creates within my sight.
I relish the view of the surging power,
For its strength is vast, its presence a tower.
Then it's time to descend once more,
And I see the boat approach the shore.
How magnificent - once again within this force!
The Rhine Falls shaping the left and right course.
I feel gratitude and calm arise,
Perhaps one day I'll return to this paradise.

My own photography

Meeting of Two Friends

In the warm sunshine, we sit here.
A relaxed evening full of pleasure.
We raise our glasses, cheer joyfully,
With alcohol-free beer, which accompanies us from now on.
The sun bathes the world in golden light.
It also affects the view of life, the sight.
Thoughts wander, worries fade away.
We simply stay in this wonderful moment.
The alcohol-free beer, so refreshing, so clear,
Brings enjoyment without regret. That's wonderful.
It sparkles on the tongue, awakens the senses,
So that one gains enjoyment and lightness.
We wait for the food, the delicious meal.
Anticipation rises. This time, it's glorious.
The aromas dance, seducing our noses,
We can't resist tasting quickly.
But in this moment, here and now,
We are simply happy without any rush.
We enjoy being together, the shared time,
And leave worries and daily life far behind.
The warm evening sky envelops us gently.
We sit together in the last sunlight.
With alcohol-free beer and good company in tow,
We forget the world. It's so far away.
So we raise our glasses to life and happiness.
Neither of us looks back.
A poem of enjoyment, of joy and peace,
In the warm sunshine, we sit here: you and I.

(Marie and Renate)

Imagine created by A.I.

Germersheim, You Beautiful Town

Germersheim, beautiful town by the Rhine,
Picturesque shores invite you to recline.
The old town with timbered frames enchants the eye,
Full of history, a piece of days gone by.
Proudly the fortress stands above the town,
So history will not be let down.
The reading café invites you to stay,
To take a break, a pleasant way.
The town's greenery fills the heart with cheer,
I'm glad I came; no regret lingers here.
I slowly wander through the old streets,
And hardly grasp the beauty my gaze meets.
Some buildings seem to speak to me,
As though history is caught here, endlessly.
Then below, the flowing stream of the Rhine -
It could hardly be more divine.
A ship lies there, tempting and fair,
But today I can't sail anywhere.
Soon I'll visit my dear friend,
For friends give life its true amend.

My own photography

Germersheim on the Rhine

On the banks of the Rhine, in its splendor bright,
Lies Germersheim by day and night.
The sun reflects in the Rhine so fair,
While soft winds gently touch the air.
The charm of times long past and gone,
Will guide you as you wander on.
The town's true beauty stands defined
By timbered houses, like art designed.
Culture and art bloom in this town on the Rhine,
Inviting me to linger for a time.
With your charm and history,
You are a place of purest magic to me.

My own photography

Father Rhine

Soft music, a bench, a table near…
Green meadows, the sun burns clear.
My friend, the Rhine, how much I've missed you!
It's so good to be with you. You give such strength, too.
I feel your energy filling the air.
To walk along your banks, I now feel the urge to dare.
I savor your strength, your steady flow.
I follow your lead - I won't let go.
Obstacles don't matter at all;
Overcoming them is natural.
It makes us strong and gives us power,
Awakening passion hour by hour.
Right now, I take a short rest
Before I go on, Father Rhine, you know best.

My own photography

Jutta

In a home full of daily duty,
Lives a soul, humble and free of vanity.
The tasks never end, yet she sees them through,
With joy in her heart, steadfast and true.
With zeal, she scrubs the kitchen clean,
Leaving each room with a polished sheen.
She washes the laundry and irons it fast,
Her work brings peace - she feels it will last.
Deep within her, a light always gleams,
As she carries the weight of daily routines.
The table is set, the meal prepared,
Her dedication shines, deeply declared.
She never rests until all is right,
Daily labor is her guiding light.
So let us honor her in this verse,
Whose strength and warmth are the universe.
Fulfillment she finds in all she does,
At evening's end, she rests because
Her heart knows peace, her soul is bright,
Satisfied after another day's light.

Alfons

You are tired
And often seek rest.
Your knees, aged by the passing days,
Can no longer carry you most of the time.
But within you lies a fighter's spirit,
Every day you're ready for sport.
Pain cannot stop you from that.
You triumph over arthritis and gout.
The years may pass you by,
But you are not one to simply lie down.
Look within yourself - the goodness that remains,
The daily joy that you experience.
The sun shines, the birds sing,
And every day will continue to bring you joy.
With courage and hope, strong and steadfast,
You will live to see what you still long for.

A Special Encounter

I started caring for you,
With uncertainty in my heart and fear too.
But now I know I'll miss it - your smile, so bright,
A source of comfort in trouble, weariness, and fright.
Like healing oil that soothes each wound,
Your smile has filled my life, like a sacred tune.
Your smile, your gaze - pure love and grace,
In silence, God's comfort shone on your face.
Your patience through hard and heavy days
Became a blessing in countless ways.
You said you had nothing left to give,
Yet you helped us all find strength to live.
By grace, I was allowed to stand by you,
To be close to your heart, faithful and true.
Our deep understanding bound us tight,
In those hard yet fulfilling nights.
The care I gave you from my heart,
Now gives me peace as you depart.
Rest now in calm and endless peace,
May eternal rest bring you release.

Imagine created by A.I.

Care

Very carefully, I enter your room.
I don't want to disturb you.
You are awake and look at me.
A glow lights up your eyes, one that cannot be described.
You have recognized me. Your smile shows it here.
Your face shines; it has longed for me.
Speaking is difficult. It's not needed.
Our hands touch, gently like a breath.
Love fills me, I don't know where from.
I bend over you. The kiss on your forehead comes easily.
Now the time has come.
We are ready
To start the day with whatever it may need.
Whatever you cannot manage, I will give as well.
We are a team,
No matter where we go.
Love from me to you,
From you to me.
I give you support, help with physical need.
Your smile heals wounds in me and feels so good.
When I leave, I am tired.
But you have given me gratitude and love.
So physically exhausted, yet so full of wealth -
Only life can do that.
A gift of awareness:
"The place where I now stand
Is right, fulfilled, and knows no pain."

Imagine created by A.I.

Where Does Your Fear Come From

At the beginning, right when we met,
You often asked, "Did I do it right?" and I just laughed.
But then I saw your eyes,
And I began to understand your deep fear inside.
Who taught you this,
That you always have to do it like this?
Uncertain, helpless, you stand before me,
Grasping my hand tightly, searching for security.
You reach for the hand that firmly holds you,
That won't push you away when you fall.
The reason why this fear drives you
Is forgotten, but what remains now
Is a feeling, a choice without memory,
A desperate search for comfort and peace.
So you hold my hand around the clock,
Even though you are safe in your own land.
Memories now slip away,
And yet you need people who love you.
I hold you tight, take you in my arms;
You rest your head on me, and I feel a warmth inside.
The little bit that I can give you now
Is comfort and courage in a forgotten life.
You are like a child who doesn't understand
Yet still reaches for the stars with open hands.
Now you are old, your life forgotten,
But you search for what I can now give you.
I am so glad to be here for you,
And your open smile rewards me too.
Have I been given a special gift,
To be able to meet you where you are in life?
Or is it simply respect and openness,
And the gift of presence, with some patience?
When I leave you at the end of the day,
I know I've left behind comfort and a little joy.

Imagine created by A.I.

Dementia

You search for words, tears running down your face.
The words you seek, you cannot trace.
Despair has now taken hold of you.
The disease has stolen your memory, too.
I feel you in your distress,
And I step into your boat, nonetheless.
I hold you close and half dazed I say
How I once struggled, lost for words one day.
Then I distract you
And ask anew:
Did you feel as a child the way I do?
We were always outside, playing free.
It was natural in the family,
To bring the children even to a feast.
Your face lights up, quick and unrestrained by forgetting.
You tell of childhood, your mother, and her cooking.
Here, there is still no forgetting.
The disease has not yet torn this away.

Much later, when I leave your side,
I see a sparkle in your eyes.
You've quickly forgotten this heavy weight,
The hurried theft of the present state.

Imagine created by A.I.

Devotion

The palm branches sway in the wind,
My eyes gaze far across the seas.
The blue, the waves, the wind, and the sea -
I see them not only with my eyes, but with my soul.
The wind and the waves take from me
The thoughts and stress that pulled me down.
The sun and the clouds in the blue sky
Have sung a song within me.
From this song, worries and thoughts quickly flee,
And within me, it grows bright once more.
I know I am in the right place in life,
Right where I can make a difference.
It often overwhelms me, and then
I lose sight of my plan.
But when peace returns, I am fulfilled
By sensing the needs of others.
And through the school of my life,
I can ease their burdens and give much.
Content am I, here and now,
That this love has been given to me.

Imagine created by A.I.

We Too Are Building the Tower of Babel
(In Our Version)

Once again.
The old songs are forgotten once again.
Once again, humanity thinks itself the greatest,
Yet it is precisely this overestimation that makes us small.
Humanity wants to be the savior of the earth.
But it is exactly this thought that leads us to ruin.
We want to accomplish it by our own strength,
Yet that only creates something greater.
They speak of love for forests,
Of care for the dear livestock.
But the most important thing has not been understood:
Only respect and reverence can promise true help.
You shouldn't just give up meat,
But also not raise an animal only for the steak.
Plants, too, have feelings and a soul,
And they suffer when I harvest them for my meal.
We were born omnivores.
So listen closely and open your ears!
If someone must suffer and die for our benefit,
We should be grateful and not use it thoughtlessly.
Avoid waste, use everything with care.
Be thankful and mindful - that's the right way to do it.
Don't throw away what deserves a second life.
Don't use toxic glue as protest - that's not what the world deserves.
Avoid the media. Go outside instead.
Pick up trash in nature - it's a disgrace.
Be aware: we are animals too.
Don't offend nature, because nature is in charge here.
For if the earth tires of our arrogance,
It will shake itself once - and humanity will be gone.
Understand it quickly, while there's still time:
Humanity is not the center of the world.
The world will survive, and so will nature.
But if we continue like this, it will be without humanity.
So learn humility, respect, and reverence.
Reflect and stop looking away.

The downfalls of past civilizations
Were caused by humanity and its arrogance.
We know the story of the Tower of Babel—and its consequences.
We're doing it again - I can feel it deep inside.

The Tower of Babel of our time
Stands on the foundation of arrogance.

Imagine created by A.I.